[for other titles and publications please see back of book]

THE RED HEIFER

THE RED HEIFER :

NUMBERS 19

JOHN METCALFE PUBLISHING TRUST

John Metcalfe Publishing Trust
Penn, Buckinghamshire

—

First published 1973
Reprinted 1980

—

Copyright John Metcalfe Publishing Trust, 1973
All rights reserved

—

ISBN 0 9502515 4 2

—

Printed by M. & A. Thomson Litho Ltd.
East Kilbride
by arrangement with HM Repros
Glasgow

—

Price 75p

J. M. P. T.

THE RED HEIFER

A Sermon from Numbers 19

vv. 1-10: **AND THE LORD** spake unto Moses and unto Aaron, saying, This is the ordinance of the law which the LORD hath commanded, saying, Speak unto the children of Israel, that they bring thee a red heifer without spot, wherein is no blemish, and upon which never came yoke: And ye shall give her unto Eleazar the priest, that he may bring her forth without the camp, and one shall slay her before his face: And Eleazar the priest shall take of her blood with his finger, and sprinkle of her blood directly before the tabernacle of the congregation seven times: And one shall burn the heifer in his sight; her skin, and her flesh, and her blood, with her dung, shall he burn: And the priest shall take cedar wood, and hyssop, and scarlet, and cast it into the midst of the burning of the heifer. Then the priest shall wash his clothes, and he shall bathe his flesh in water, and afterward he shall come into the camp, and the priest shall be unclean until the even. And he that burneth her shall wash his clothes in water, and bathe his flesh in water, and shall be unclean until the even. And a man that is clean shall gather up the ashes of the heifer, and lay them up without the camp in a clean place, and it shall be kept for the congregation of the children of Israel for a water of separation: it is a purification for sin. And he that gathereth the ashes of the heifer shall wash his clothes, and be unclean until the even: and it shall be unto the children of Israel, and unto the stranger that sojourneth among them, for a statute for ever.

---

vv. 11-16: **HE THAT** toucheth the dead body of any man shall be unclean seven days. He shall purify himself with it on the third day, and on the seventh day he shall be clean: but if he purify not himself the third day, then the seventh day he shall not be clean. Whosoever toucheth the dead body of any man that is dead, and purifieth not himself, defileth the tabernacle of the LORD; and that soul shall be cut off from Israel: because the water of separation was not sprinkled upon him, he shall be unclean; his uncleanness is yet upon him. This is the law, when a man dieth in a tent: all that come into the tent, and all that is in the tent, shall be unclean seven days. And every open vessel, which hath no covering bound upon it, is unclean. And whosoever toucheth one that is slain with a sword in the open fields, or a dead body, or a bone of a man, or a grave, shall be unclean seven days.

---

vv. 17-22: **AND FOR** an unclean person they shall take of the ashes of the burnt heifer of purification for sin, and running water shall be put thereto in a vessel: And a clean person shall take hyssop, and dip it in the water, and sprinkle it upon the tent, and upon all the vessels, and upon the persons that were there, and upon him that touched a bone, or one slain, or one dead, or a grave: And the clean person shall sprinkle upon the unclean on the third day, and on the seventh day: and on the seventh day he shall purify himself, and wash his clothes, and bathe himself in water, and shall be clean at even. But the man that shall be unclean, and shall not purify himself, that soul shall be cut off from among the congregation, because he hath defiled the sanctuary of the LORD: the water of separation hath not been sprinkled upon him; he is unclean. And it shall be a perpetual statute unto them, that he that sprinkleth the water of separation shall wash his clothes; and he that toucheth the water of separation shall be unclean until even. And whatsoever the unclean person toucheth shall be unclean; and the soul that toucheth it shall be unclean until even.

*   *   *   *

THE RED HEIFER

We are going to have a cursory and simple view of the red heifer as seen in the nineteenth chapter of the fourth book of Moses called Numbers.

The chapter divides naturally into three parts. The first is from verses 1-10 and is the provision made for when death comes into the camp. The second, verses 11-16, is the reason or the necessity for the provision, and the third, from verses 17-22, is the application or the method of the provision.

It is a remarkable truth that in Exodus we see God's approach to that seed which he had before separated in the book of Genesis. God approaches his people whom he foreknew and whom he had set apart in Abraham. Exodus therefore is God's approach to man in Israel. Leviticus on the other hand is Israel's approach in man to God, and it makes known the manner—and the only manner—in which man can come before God, doing so in an external pictorial and figurative form.

However, those outward signs, these symbols and types, are so carefully delineated and devoid of human imagination that it was said to Moses, See that thou make all things according to the pattern which was shown thee in the mount. Take care! And therefore we see in a graphic picture form the manner in which God is approached by Levi set forth in the figures of the true in the book of Leviticus, just as we see graphically set forth in the book of Exodus God's approach to Israel by Moses.

3

However, when it comes to Numbers, we discover the testimony of God in man: the testimony of God in Israel is clearly set forth. Numbers sets forth distinctly and in many ways the Levitical service and various other truths of God's testimony in and among a people; not least of course is the fact that he numbers the people. That is not a prerogative David can take upon himself. God numbers the people. God is jealous of his people. There is an offering for jealousy, and it has to do with a woman. That he views his people as a bride is clearly to be deduced.

Numbers is a wonderful book; we see that when God establishes his testimony in a people they are already a separated people. He has approached them. They are continually approaching him. They are in communication and communion with him in a way that is knowledgeable—the priest's lips should keep knowledge. They are knowledgeable, they are instructed, they are a gathered people. And we find in the book of Numbers that God's testimony is established in the midst of this people who have been approached by God, who do approach God, and who are gathered to him.

We find that they are a transitory people. They go on from station to station, as they go from strength to strength journeying towards Zion. They are a journeying people. They are a pilgrim people. They are a distinct people. They are moving out of the world. They are moving out of the world's city. They are moving out of the world's state. They are in soul separation from it in a figure. They really are a peculiar people. They are a people who are distinct, and they are a people who are united. Their backs are to the world, their faces are towards the testimony in the midst of them, their feet walk according to the pillar of cloud and fire before them, and their hearts are set on the heavenly land yet to be manifested unto them.

They are a people completely separate; there is nothing

4

but a wilderness all around them. Then there is their camp, and their tribes are in special places in their tents, each tribe having its place around the central tent or tabernacle of God in the midst, and each going up in its times and seasons. It is God going with a people. And this is of course a figure of the true church of God—a figure to which the church should answer.

Once the church is established, the most effective mode of evangelism is by the saints being that church which God has made them through the gospel: by their being true worshippers. More than anything else this will attract the thoughtful and perceptive. The modern method that you must get nearer and nearer the world outside the church, and yet moralise and talk more and more down to them inside it, is absolutely ridiculous; and in any event an insult to intelligence. We should be what we are. There is never, in the world or out of it, the warrant for being unnatural, stilted or pompous, or putting on special airs and graces or manners. If a man is not sincere and guileless, either in sin or out of it, he is not worth much.

However, we see here the people in Numbers, the testimony of God established in man, and we find God numbering the people. What a wonderful thing that is! What numbers were numbered! Another thing we see is that they are numbered as able to go to war. They had to fight for this position: it is not maintained by pacifism, nor is it maintained by singular heroes. It is maintained by a unified people, humbly walking together with a real militant zeal for the defence and maintenance of the gospel and of the testimony which has gathered them. They must have the courage and the strength to go to war at the cost probably of their life, which is the danger of war.

They are numbered—the order of the tribes in their tents is seen in chapter 2. The Levites' service follows—indeed, the book might well be called The Service. Then there is the question of the so-called 'redemption' money, or as it should be called, ransom money. There is no such thing as redemption money. As if you could buy redemption! I never heard such nonsense as that foolish notion. The price of redemption is blood, not silver, and it never was silver or gold—what a vain tradition! It is ransom; not ransom for the redemption of the soul, but ransom for the failure of redeemed souls to rise to the service of sonship. That was why they paid their due over against the Levites who were chosen in their place. Then we get the age and the time of the Levites' service, we get the number of the Kohathites, and the trial of jealousy—what a tremendous thing that is! Then comes the blessing of the people, the offerings of the princes, the journeys, the quails, Miriam's leprosy, and so on and so forth. And then after the priests' and Levites' portions, we come eventually to the water of separation and the red heifer.

One of the questions that might arise is, Why is this sacrifice not with the other sacrifices in the book of Leviticus? What is the force of this? The answer is it is a sacrifice in connection with the position that obtains in the book of Numbers, concerning the congregation of the Lord's people. It is a sacrifice for a redeemed and ransomed people in the service in a certain circumstance which is set forth in the context of the book of Numbers; the context being that God has come to a people whom he foreknew, the seed of Abraham, has gathered that people, and has then caused that people to approach him as seen heretofore, in order that they might serve God in a way of sonship: 'Let my son go that he may serve me;' 'Out of Egypt have I called my son.'

In order for them to approach him, he has established a tabernacle for the way of worship to be among them; they have approached him and now they are journeying with this tabernacle and surrounding this tent with which, by a Levitical and priestly service, they are journeying as men of war guarding what they have received. They are journeying through the wilderness, and one of the things they must do as guarding what they have received of God as a redeemed people with the testimony among them is, they must have the waters of separation available on the perimeter of the camp.

Because if you could have looked as an angel down from heaven and seen spiritually, what you would have seen is the whole world in thick darkness, the outer darkness, and one pool of light illuminating as with an unearthly ethereal glow the midst of the camp by the light of this glory, shining and bathing with light up to the perimeter of the camp. Right to the extremity of the camp it is light. And outside it is total darkness. That is the moral picture. And that light is alive with a living people, and everywhere outside it in and of the world there are walking corpses. Zombies in the dark! But in that one radiant circle is a living free-born people walking in the light and full of light, life and love.

The people inside that pool of light are full of vigour and life. They are healthy, energetic, vibrant with a life which is not their own—God is in the camp. God will not have his people with the atmosphere of death among them. We should never diminish the truth of the church because of the truths of the compassions and grace of the Saviour to the lost and dead—that does not make the church lost and dead or excuse its being so! For the One who finds, quickens, gathers, and brings in to the living fold, is he who makes a people whose name is 'holiness to the Lord' both found, alive, and together as one in light and life in the Lord.

Every single church ought to have one source of existence namely, God the Father and the Lord Jesus Christ in the gospel ministered by the Spirit. One should be in real unity with them that have such, and refuse it with them that have not, and should answer locally to such a reflection.

7

The neighbourhood should be a pool of darkness as to religion, as to God, and the church should be one pool of light in a gathered people, a gathered congregation; God in the midst sending forth the light from his living presence in the midst of the church; and this area of light being the one area also of living men before God, the world being in darkness and death even until now. That is the picture you get.

And in order to its being maintained, a provision is made in this context and in this book, and that provision is called, The waters of separation which are a purification for sin. It is in this context that the provision of the red heifer obtains. What is it for? It is for this: if someone should inadvertently or advertently fall into a way of death—moral, internal death—and come into contact with it so as to be defiled by it, that person is out. Out! Because this is an area of light and life, and dark and death just do not belong here. Morally speaking death is not of it. Contact with death is not viewed as arbitrary, it is seen as moral. But if not arbitrary, neither is God merciless with the defiled; provision is made.

It is not the will of God that any of these should perish or abide in darkness. It is his will rather to maintain them in light and life. It is not the will of God that these should remain dead, for the Son of God is come and hath abolished death, and brought life and immortality to light through the gospel. So therefore a provision is made for one of the congregation, or for any of the congregation, or for any coming into the congregation, to maintain the life that distinguishes that congregation, and alone warrants its being called the congregation of the Lord.

What precious truths are gathered up in the church! Unity is in its very nature the conjoining of separate units. The whole conception on from Genesis, when Eve was built from Adam, to the ark, to the tabernacle, to being baptised into one body, is of one Spirit, one Lord, one faith, one

8

baptism, one God and Father of all: the very idea of any independency is alien! Rather a living loving vibrant Spirit-filled people, for God has come down with a witness and dwells among them.

The real features that made them a people of God were not the furniture nor the tabernacle! Do you understand? Those real features are not the furniture of the tent with which people are so enamoured, not the pins, nor the poles, not the skins, nor the laver, not that which intrigues curious minds, nor the form of Levitical service, or which sacrifice is which. Those things are not the things which really are the criteria which distinguish the people. The criteria which distinguish the people are light and life and love in the Lord: without these features men divide over signs.

Although today, most mistake the youthful enthusiasm of natural life for spiritual life! and I may add, not only mistake but many exploit youth's gullibility in the modern cult of and obsession with the young, cruelly exploiting their ignorance and vulnerability. Youth is naturally generative and has a spontaneous zeal and energy which has the appearance of life. But life before God is another thing; it is eternal life, and if eternal life, then where is the life of yesterday's youth today? It is all very well being obsessed with today's youth, and for the ageing one can understand the infatuation: it is a deceptive form of substitution, pleasantly diverting for the dead old hypocrite in Zion!

However the test is not youth but time; and one is tried when in time responsibilities come: not when as a youngster one has a headful of untried ideals and a heart bursting with life that may or may not prove to be spiritual. Time will tell, because what is eternal is the one thing time cannot affect. With eternal life, one goes on bearing fruit in old age; one has the dew of one's youth from the womb of the morning. But whilst young, it is a time to be quiet and

9

learn. In scripture it is old men, old women, young men, young women, children, masters and servants. That is 'the household of faith', all in the proper order.

Life is far more weighty than youthful enthusiasm. The man that has life is like a tree planted by the rivers of water, he bringeth forth his fruit in his season and his leaf fadeth never. Got that? Never, never! That is life. And look at the issues of that life! The ungodly are not so. They are 'like the chaff which the wind driveth away.' So much movement, so much activity, so chaffy, so light, so flippant, and so carried to and fro by every wind of doctrine.

But the life that is of God leads to the fear of God, to a deep solemn reverence for the truth, to divine understanding into the word. It has a real grasp of Father, Son and Holy Ghost, and no room is left for death. However, inadvertently one may touch death and be defiled. What then? Provision is made for recovery in the event of that life being defiled. You agree with that, do you? It's obvious, isn't it? And the provision is made in a red heifer.

It is a question of death as it relates to the whole living congregation. Whoso toucheth the dead body of any man that is dead and purifieth not himself, defileth the tabernacle of the Lord. Of course, we have heard some of these ridiculous clerics, and we have seen some of these ludicrous commentaries that theological professors put out, and you would think it was a school of hygiene, not the camp of God. Oh well, they say, the reason is hygiene. How ridiculous! How absolutely contemptible! Hygienic! I ask you! If I touch a man that has just died, am I going to need seven days to get clean from it? Undertakers do it all the time, don't they? If I touch a dry bone of a dead man, dead perhaps two hundred years, am I going to catch something for seven days? It is a figure, a type of the true! It is simply that even the remotest connection with death morally has no place before God and in the congregation of his people: that is the realm of light and life!

They are a living people. They are not a backward-looking 'once-saved-always-saved' people. They are not a one-decision people. They are not a one-act-of-faith people. Life is not something like a kind of a force that you switch on and flick off and then forever pretend it has stayed on! Life is something that pulses round the body with the constant beating of the heart, and it maintains in life that body vitally, vibrantly, and actively—life is something that goes on. Isn't it? In its nature. And this is a people that are alive. How wonderful this truth is, and what a wonderful thing when you can find a living people.

How many years have I spent since I have been born of God wandering round from church to church, congregation to congregation, assembly to assembly, denomination to denomination, or to no denomination, seeking a *living people*, and how rare it is to see the signs of it, although maybe you do find a person here, a person there, or even perhaps a tiny group that is alive within a dead congregation —that is the most you can find today. But a living people maintained in a way of life, all of them alive, all of them with their drawn swords in their hands like mighty men round Solomon's bed and couch, determined to maintain this place as a living place—I never found it.

What I did find was a very few scattered individuals sweetly alive, wonderfully alive, though how they were kept alive, I do not know. A few in a congregation here, more in a congregation there, one in a congregation, astonishingly, somewhere else; but not a people that were alive, characterised by the life of God, everlasting life, in the whole congregation dwelling in an atmosphere of light and life. It is a wonderful thing if you can find such a people: you cherish them.

So much so does God cherish this and seek such to worship him, that defilement comes from no more than even the touching of a long-dead man after he has decayed

11

and is reduced to bones, which takes time you will admit! even walking over a grave, it's enough to defile! God is, as I may so speak, so wary that anything should spoil this which he loves and cherishes that even the remote touch of a vapour, such as the tainted atmosphere in an open vessel, must be eliminated!—it wouldn't do any harm in itself, but it might lead to something that does; if you become familiar with the circumference and the things that do not matter, how easy it is then to wander into the centre and trifle with the real dangers—if you touch a bone, you are unclean. If you touch a grave, you are unclean.

You may say that is lack of logic. But I say, No! For one thing, if God does it it must be logical, it must be you that cannot see it; that is on principle. And for a second thing, I deny it is lack of logic; it is wise, because in my experience people, especially the young, love to dare to do something and hate to be restrained by their elders and betters. And out of sight they will put forth their hand, and whilst fear and even respect for God will stop them doing what is really bad, if they can play with the fringes they will. But if they put their hands into a dangerous area, which they think does not matter, there is an evil invisible hand the other side that will grip them. And when that happens their hand will never be let go as far as it lies with the tempter, the wicked one, no, not world without end.

Therefore God makes it such that even the circumference —a grave, a bone—cannot be touched. There is no room for death. God looks for a living people to be kept alive. He separated them by blood. There is a ring of blood round this camp, and outside that ring of blood it is black. And inside it is bathed in a beautiful soft light. Outside it is dead; inside it is all alive with a life so potent it can raise the dead and carry over to everlasting glory. And anybody that crossed over into the darkness to dally, why, they trampled underfoot the blood of Christ wherewith they were sanctified. So you see how important it is that the saints should be kept alive and living with a people of God.

Now this cannot be undertaken in respect of a whole people the world over, as though all the churches answered to the one camp and we were all gathered together in one place as they were; the churches are not so. Israel was a national entity in a defined geographical location outside of which was none of Israel, and beyond which was no other religious location. The churches are called out of every nation and all localities to meet in congregation. Hence any application of these truths must be spiritual not literal. Literal? How ridiculous! How could it happen? The answer is it could happen only through a totally wrong conception of and attitude about the church.

Each congregation is responsible before God to answer to these truths, neither is it possible nor is it practicable, for one congregation or person in it to impose on another. You can't do it. It was not done even in the early church. John the apostle says, I wrote unto the church: but Diotrephes, who loveth to have the preeminence among them, receiveth us not. There are some things you must suffer. And you cannot bring in the glory yet in this scene. But you can and you ought morally to answer yourself, and to answer with a people. And if a people will not answer with you, you should leave them if it is morally impossible to go on. Because it is a moving position—from camp to camp. And moreover that is the testimony of the people of God—they have done this. That is what I believe and hold. But you cannot impose on others without dictatorship. You must in the end leave others, no matter who they are, to the Lord's judgment. And believe me, he does judge!

I say therefore the answer to this truth is the onus on every individual to find such a people, and it is the onus upon every people in view of the Lord's love that they should be in a living area, and within the circumference and sphere, as it were, of life in the Lord. That they should be together and should maintain life, that they should have

13

their swords drawn and ready to defend the gospel and uphold this life and light and love that is the characteristic of the church of God. Even the touch of a bone brought in death.

Do you follow? Surely that is correct, isn't it? I think you must admit that it is correct. And although in this case it was all the people, in our case it is not. For instance I cannot influence the church in Australia—I don't know anything about them. If they write to me and say there is an argument between two assemblies as to which has the table, that is none of my business. It is between them and the Lord. I am not one of the angels or one of the twenty-four elders looking down on the whole situation. Then I can judge over all the earth, when I am over all the earth. But when I am in Tylers Green, all I can judge is what surrounds me. And it is not for me to occupy myself with things too high for me. And that in my opinion was the mistake, though a sincere one, which led to a division at a certain time. Mind you, as has been said, only the good wood splits, the rotten just crumbles into a featureless heap! So I would rather have good split wood than the kind of evangelical sawdust indifference you get from a people who have not got enough conviction to do anything except lifelessly merge by force of gravity.

I think it is necessary to say that, because your mind may be quick and you may say to me: Well, it is all very well, but how can you answer to this today because where is the people who all have this intent? I answer, I don't know. I never found them. But I know this, through many travails and sorrows and soul-suffering over many many years I have desired these things, and have been kept alive and drawn by the Lord, and in some measure in the fruits of my own ministry I have certainly found them. And I can only say, Seek and ye shall find. But don't try and create because it is not your prerogative. And whilst you should judge righteous judgment, I tell you this—it is another fault

14

that is so easy—don't try and judge things too high for you, or beyond your capacity or anyone's capacity to do anything about. We are not called to judge with the judgment of God over the whole church. We cannot do it. We are called to judge with the judgment of men to keep ourselves alive, and alive with the people of God in a given place devoid of error and darkness. And beyond that, who can go? We cannot. And it only leads to mental chaos if not downright collapse if we attempt to do so. I know, I have tried. I can assure you it is more than just theory to me.

Right. We have this position, then, and I think it is clear to us. The point is this, the people of God are not in any way permitted to come into contact with death. Here was the necessity: verse 14, This is the law, when a man dieth in a tent: all that come into the tent, and all that is in the tent, shall be unclean seven days. You did not even have to touch him, if he died in your presence it was enough. And every open vessel which hath no covering bound upon it is unclean. That atmosphere is so subtle, so deadly, so noxious, and yet so imperceptible in its coming over you, that even if a vessel is there into which the atmosphere can drift like a kind of invisible miasma, then it has got to be treated as unclean. And, oh, how subtly the atmosphere of death can be brought into a meeting through one vessel.

Sometimes the apostles call our bodies vessels; Paul says we have this treasure in earthen vessels. And you can come into contact with death by walking in the counsel of the religious ungodly, by standing in the way of evangelical sinners, and sitting in the seat of the theological scorner, can't you? You can form worldly friendships, can't you? Says James, Know ye not that the friendship of the world is enmity with God? And because your vessel is too open and accessible your whole conversation is thus pervaded by the worldly—though religious!—friendship: death creeps in; it's not of Christ, is it? It's not of the Spirit, is it? It's not of life, is it? It's not of the gospel, is it? It's not of spiritual

15

experience, is it? It's not in the language of Zion, is it? You can't say that that man was *born* there, can you? And so your vessel becomes filled with this will-o'-the-wisp grey wraith of death from your contact.

You come into the meeting, oh, but you have got to speak differently here, haven't you? You know the words you should speak here, and this smoke is getting at the word and is pervading the atmosphere, now. Certainly it is rarefied. It is thinning. But it gets in! And it is simply the dead spirit that is giving out the dead letter that killeth. And you can feel it is just the voice of words. You can feel it is all endearments to Christ. I have sat in a meeting not very far from here and I have heard people mouthing endearments to Christ, and I have felt as if somebody got a sledge-hammer and slammed it down on my soul, so bruised was I with shock and misery. And I believe I did not feel that; I believe that was the impression of the Spirit. Of a natural man making spiritual sounds about Christ. Honey! There shall be no honey. The cloying sick-sweet produce of fleshly sentiment! There shall be no honey with this sacrifice, Lev. 2:11. Salt, yes.

Death! You see that, don't you? Every open vessel. Had it been covered it would have been all right, wouldn't it? But there was no covering, it was too open, too liberal, too broad, anything could get in, and it did; then it is unclean. A little of this dreadfully old-fashioned narrowness would have helped, wouldn't it?! A little covering of separation, eh? Not even the risk of it coming in then, it is true, isn't it? And whoever touches one that is slain with a sword in the open fields, or a dead body, or a bone of a man, or a grave, well, he is unclean, you know.

People used to say of the much maligned early Nonconformists, that they were much too narrow when they began. Oh, were they just? Well, they would not even go and hear so-and-so preach. Wouldn't they? Well, perhaps they judged that so-and-so was a Pharisee. And perhaps they were right. There was a very great possibility of their being right, I should think. Why cannot they go and hear a Pharisee? Woe unto you, ye Pharisees, for ye are as graves which appear not, says Christ. Do you say he may have been a brother as well? This he appears not, to you! Woe unto you Pharisees, you are as graves, says Jesus. *Graves!* And I read this, Whosoever toucheth a dead body, or a bone of a man, or a *grave*, shall be unclean seven days.

There is a certain moral onus upon the living. Says the prophet, The living, the living, he shall praise thee as I do this day! But you have got to protect life. And the way to protect it is separation. That is what is before us, The water of separation. But, verse 21: And it shall be a perpetual statute unto them, that he that sprinkleth the water of separation shall wash his clothes; and he that toucheth the water of separation shall be unclean until even. Why? Because even though that water of separation is so clean that it cleanses, as from death, yet as you sprinkle it the water, touching your finger, goes in an arc and touches the unclean person: there is contact! The arc of water reaches and joins together in the instant before it cleanses. That is enough! Unclean!

That is how alive we should be, my friends and brethren, is it not so? We should really be alive. We should not have a name to live—I know thy works, Christ says of this church, that thou hast a name that thou livest and art dead —we should really be alive. And the whole church; it is not a question of me being alive. It is not a question of brother X being alive, or sister Y being alive; this is an ordinance for *them.* It is a people that is the whole congregation, and this great picture of the whole people of God in the church should be reflected in the church that was at Corinth, the church that was at Thessalonica, the church that was in Judea. They should all reflect this, and that is what gives them their unity. They all answer to the same truth; not

17

that people impose it on them, or some central assembly somewhere says, Do this, and they all do it.

The necessity for the sacrifice lay in the fact that—notwithstanding all carefulness—death will come in inadvertently ever and anon among a living people of God. Verses 11-16 deal with the fact that he that touches the dead body of a man shall be unclean seven days. It is the law that if a man dies in the tent, everything in that tent shall be unclean seven days. Whoever touches a bone of a man, one that is slain, a grave, he is unclean. It is death. One will come into contact with it, and of course the wages of sin is death. It is not sin, it is the consequence of sin—death. The problem is the defilement of death, because to that there is a reaction from the living God.

But what is to be done about it? To treat it as though it were the norm for Christians to be defiled, or even to go on sinning? Certainly that is not touching death inadvertently, it is earning it and bringing it down morally! 'These things write I unto you that ye sin not.' 'Sin shall not have dominion over you, for ye are not under the law but under grace.' 'Be ye holy, for I am holy,' saith the Lord. Death! It will come in, not here because of sin, but inadvertently through contact, as defiling; but there is a provision made for it among the people of God and the congregation of God.

What I want you to notice from the fact that—despite all care—death will appear and cause contact among a people of God, is how objectionable death was. First of all it must be kept outside Israel: the waters of separation; and secondly it must not be near the Lord or be brought into his presence: the waters of purification. Because it says in verse 9, It shall be kept for the congregation of the children of Israel for a water of separation: it is a purification for sin; hence so foul is this defilement that although the defiled person did no moral wrong, he touched death,

18

and it is called sin. The water of purification is to keep it from the presence of the Lord, and the water of separation to keep it from the congregation of the people of Israel. Because whosoever toucheth a dead body, a bone, a grave, defileth the tabernacle of the Lord; so I say, it must be kept outside of Israel and it must not be near the Lord.

Why? Because death is regarded as an enemy. In Hebrews 2:14 we read, Him that had the power of death, that is the devil. Death is not inanimate. It was not for nothing that through some superstitious instinct the great novelists of times past have depicted death as a bony shrouded messenger. They have embodied death as a ghastly, grisly last visitor. One of the best tracts I ever read was by a man called C. A. Coates entitled 'A Preacher of the Old School', and in it death is depicted as though he were an animate person. But in a certain sense—not that death is animate or there is a person called death—the fact, the atmosphere, the reality of death is pervaded by a living intelligence. It is activated by a real being. He that hath the power of death, that is the invisible, the intangible, the all-but-unknown spirit called the devil: a real being.

That is why the apostle Paul in the Corinthian epistle says, The last *enemy* to be destroyed is death. Death is depicted as an enemy, not as a happening, not as a mischance, not as a misfortune, not as a terminal unit, but as an enemy. Now to be an enemy, it must be an intelligently directed activity, and an activity alien to those against whom it is directed. If so, death is something that is contrary to me, that is against me, that is determined to destroy me: it is the enemy.

I say, moreover, man was not created to die. Death is, in fact, not only pervaded by Satan, not only in itself an enemy, but it is unnatural. Man was not created to die. Life was not intended to be terminated at the end of sixty or seventy years. Man was not created for that: he was created for immortality. When Adam was put in the garden of Eden, do you think God intended him to rot and moulder in the most disgusting and degrading way after eighty or ninety years? Does God pronounce man very good and then after sixty years make him a wrinkled bag of withered skin and dried-up flesh, to be laid in the grave and eaten by worms? Is that natural? Have you ever seen a corpse? Have you ever uncovered a corpse? How awful! It is unnatural.

Life is natural. One should grow up and attain a vigour, one should in that vigour attain the prudence of maturity, and the increase of one's life should then reach a point where it no longer makes one's brain or one's body grow bigger, but it should maintain without decay the substance in which that life dwells, namely the body. The reason this does not happen is because of the fall of Adam. Death has come in. Death is pervaded by Satan, death is an enemy, death is unnatural, and finally death is a judgment.

Where did it come from? It came as the result and is the inexorable consequence of sin—the wages of sin is death. Not only physical death; physical death results from moral death! It is because your life has not got the strength to overcome and conquer the decaying influences in the body, brain and vital substances that you die. Christ's life has got the vigour to prevent this decay and death. He hath the power of an endless life, mark it, the *power* of an endless life. From the womb of the morning he has the dew of his youth. If he exerts the power of that life in the presence of any substance, however decayed, it cannot remain so. His life is too strong: Lazarus, come forth! I will, be thou clean. Arise, take up thy bed and walk. I AM the resurrection and the life!

Originally, Adam's life, whilst of course not possessed innately with the powerful divine virtue that is in Christ, was innocent of inbred sin, that seedbed of death. But after the fall neither he nor his posterity maintained this purity,

20

because of the curse of indwelling sin. By one man inbred sin entered into the world, and death by it, for the corruption of indwelling sin of itself is the cause of death by decay in the race. This is the judgment of God.

Therefore sin is a condemnation on the race, and death is its seal. It shows that we are a fallen race; we had been on probation in Adam, Adam fell, and the race fell in him. The race therefore is fallen into corruption, conceived in sin, already with the judgment passed upon it before birth, already with the power of death so strong in human nature that death is certain, from birth, to overcome that life. Doom is written on every living thing. No one ever will have—this side of death—the strength to prevent decay and the strength to prevent the oncoming judgment of the grave.

Once I saw an old lady fight death as I never thought to see it fought. She had virtually died but she hung on with sheer will-power. And I saw how, as I sat at the bedside of that woman in a coma, day after day she hung on. She would not move, she could hardly move, but she was not going to leave that body, and with the strength of an indomitable will—there are not many like that any more!—with the strength of an indomitable will, she was not going to let go. We could do with some of these people with a will like that. That is called character. It was an old-fashioned thing that used to happen in Victorian times! But she was not going to let go. And I remember after days when you thought she had gone, she would just lift up a clawed hand and you could feel the determination in her. She hung on long after that; she was conquered at last.

For one cannot win. Not one of Adam's race can defeat the last enemy. Only the Last Adam can do that. And he is the One with the power of an endless life. He is the one to beat that enemy, and if he does not beat that enemy for you that enemy will beat you, and beat you down to the grave, and beat you down to outer darkness, and beat you into utter, eternal and awful misery.

Well, let me come to the next point, namely, mark the salvation set forth in the red heifer. The thing is that we are not really dealing with deliverance from the fall of sin and death. What we are dealing with is a people who have already been delivered; but through sin, or through worldly associations—deadly connections, worldly religious associations—become involved with death, or through contact with the consequences of sin, have become defiled. Their open vessel even, no more than that, has got the atmosphere and they bring it in. They should shut up for seven days, for it is for seven days that they shall be shut up.

Where is the church with the courage to say to a man who is normally spiritual but who has obviously gone dead for a season, Brother, you ought to be quiet for a few days till you have got before the Lord in a way of purification and separation and you are right again, because things are not coming out alive but dead? Can you tell me? But it should be so, and it has been so. And moreover, in days of grace and love in the church the brother would turn round and say, Thank you, brother. Yes, let us see that the Lord has set forth salvation in the form of a red heifer among his people for the time when death may come into the church. That is why you should never force a man to pray, never put him in a position where he must speak perforce: there is a time—oh, so sadly—there is a time of shutting up.

If you are touched of death inadvertently, suffer your discipline and go morally where they had to go literally—outside the camp. For seven days or more if need be. More than you need is provided and that provision was made before you were born. Therefore as such, as a gathered people, as one body to reflect the glory of Christ in a yielding, meek and living way seek grace to help in time of need. Yet nevertheless what is lacking is not necessarily life, but may be faith to realise the life given: spiritual, priestly discernment is required.

Why a heifer? Well, it is feminine—the heifer; it is

the substitute ordained of God for death in the daughter of Jerusalem. I would say this is the people of God as regarded in Romans seven, figuratively a woman bound by the law to her husband; the people there are seen as a woman, as a bride, as one whom Christ seeks for himself to answer in affectionate love to his husbandship and lordship. If we should turn our back on our husband and so affect death towards him, and worse than that, when we have turned our face and back on our husband and have just cut him off, we then mutter endearments, don't you think that warrants sacrifice? For I do. What a way to treat your husband! Is that love? That is death come in. You are dead to him. It is wifely affection refused, or given by lip service on the part of the bride without heart-yielding.

I have espoused you a chaste virgin unto Christ, says Paul. And yet how often they went a-whoring after false gods. Dead! And yet whilst a-whoring they drew near the Lord with their lips, though their heart was far from him. Oh, they all come, and if it is a meeting for worship or round the table we have all got to say something, haven't we? Or else Mr. So-and-so is hired for so much a year and must speak at the required rate, and that is that. So they say it, even if their hearts are far from him, or their souls utterly dead. Well, that is all right, it is what always has been done, isn't it? As your fathers did, so do ye. I say that is a-whoring against Christ. It is speaking out of a vessel of death. It never proceeded from the heart much less the Spirit; it cannot pass the conscience, much less the judgment seat of Christ. And it needs a substitute, and since the people say Amen, it is all one. It has affected the whole people. They are all in it. Guilty! Instead of having the character to shut their mouth, no, to please the brother or so as not to give offence, Amen, they all say.

How often this goes on, and it goes on, and it goes on, and it goes on, and in the end Christ says, I will remove thy candlestick out of its place. A death permanent. Fallen in the wilderness! And that is what has happened today. It is dead. It has got the words of salvation inherited from a once-living people, but it never got the life. And it won't do, you know. It is death. Anyone that can smell death knows it: it may have a biblical shroud, but it stands in the dead letter that killeth. It is not the letter that giveth life, rather it commits to burial. Many go as far as scripture, they search the scriptures, but they do not come to the Life. It is spirituality rather than accuracy that is lacking: dead! Not that there is much accuracy either!

Yes, the red heifer is necessary, because it is not just me, it is us. It is not just you, it is us. You are going to affect me and I am going to affect you: we are one body in the Lord. And I know it comes in with me and it comes in with you. Let's be quiet. Let's wait till it has passed over. Let us wait on the Lord—an excellent practice—bow our heads and keep quiet. Ride the storm out until you feel the peace. Then come in and you feel the witness within. It is a great thing to walk by a witness, my friends. It is a mark of the spiritual; they do not walk by the letter, they walk by the Spirit—it is confirmed by the letter. Then you can open your mouth again. Is that right? Yes. I believed, therefore I spake.

Well, it is the people of God as the bride of Christ, isn't it? We should reflect that precious truth, shouldn't we? We should be a bride to him, a chaste virgin to him. Not go a-whoring back to the gods we had the other side of the flood. Not play the harlot after false gods with worldly affections, should we? No, no, we should be Christ's. Hearken O daughter, and consider, and incline thine ear; forget also thy father's house. And be a pure true chaste virgin, a real bride of Christ, my dear people.

A heifer being a female sacrifice answers in the feminine to what that people should have been, but were not. Therefore it is a reflection of what they were not that is

24

displayed, and it is feminine. That is what they were not—feminine. It is the purely feminine counterpart that is marred, ruined and collapsed through death. It is the Spirit of life in Christ Jesus who brings in this feminine, wifely, bridal response, the yearning for his return, the intuition, the softness, the gentle femininity, the whispering 'Come, Lord Jesus!'

As regards its being a red heifer, I can perceive several things here. The first is that red is the colour of vigour, health and life. My beloved, says the bride in Song of Solomon, is red—he is ruddy. He is full of vigour and life. Well, that is what was needed—a dead whore brought to penitence, a live virgin heifer is her substitute to answer to her defilement. I say it is healthy and alive and able to die vicariously, and present that life as dead in the place of that dead life. This heifer as the feminine counterpart stands in righteousness and lives in life. But the collapse of sin and the burial of death have crept in and are affecting everything. It is not necessarily one's own contact with death, it might have crept in from outside. But everyone becomes defiled, and instead of 'come out of her, my people' it is 'I will spew thee out of my mouth.'

Moreover, I would say another thing about the word red. Because there are no vowels in ancient Hebrew, simply consonants, the word 'red' can either be rendered Adam or Edom. It is *dm*. The word for blood incidently is dam, the word for red. Adam was taken from the red earth—his name was called Adam. Adamah is one of the words for earth. Now take Adam—by one man sin entered into the world and death by sin, and so death passed upon all men, for in that one man, Adam, all fell. He was a man of the earth, the first man was of the earth, Adam, earthy.

It has an answer to when nature gets into the church, and when the flesh gets into what is spiritual; when fallen nature conceives it brings forth sin and when sin is

25

complete it brings forth the work of judgment, it brings out death. And the answer is to get back to the root and judge the fall in the cause. From natural sentiment there cannot be true wifely and real bridal affection for Christ. We have got to be brought by the Spirit who moved Rebecca and taken out of that place, and out of the old connections by way of substitutionary death, and be brought in a new realm of life into a new country on a new basis, to bring forth fruit unto God as Abraham's living seed.

As regards Edom, which is the same word for red, Edom is the habitation of Esau. It is known as the habitation of pride, and you may be sure pride goes before a fall. Pride! Pride goes before a fall, doesn't it? Or else you have been converted long enough now. Why, when you were first converted words bubbled out rather like a baby to start with, but how sweet the sound of a new convert's first breath. When we first heard him pray, was it not moving? But then they begin to catch on a word—ah, that was a good phrase, let's have that. And then we can really do it, can't we? Quite professional, isn't it? Of course, we are against clericalism, but we can manage the professional roll-out, can't we? Like one of those things they had in Victorian times with holes in, you turned a handle and it played a tune and the keys went down. I don't know what you call them. But so it is in many an evangelical meeting. Tinkle, tinkle, tinkle! Tinkling brass and a clanging cymbal. Sounding brass and hath not love—nothing! Spontaneity has gone, enthusiasm is lost. Pride! You have got something to rely on, something to fall back on, you see. Resources!

Another thing about Edom is that it was where Esau dwelt. And Esau was the first-born. It was Jacob, Israel, who was the second-born, who supplanted the first. And this substitutionary red heifer indicates to me that death has come in by the first man again, that nature has been applied to, that the flesh has been given place to. But I tell you the people of God are a people who should walk in the

Spirit of life. They have been born of God and out of their bellies should flow rivers of living water. That should be our experience in measure. Of course, measure differs, as God has dealt to every man the gift. It is a living place, my friends. Life characterises them. A well of water springs up—mark that, *springs up*—unto everlasting life.

Very well, that is the red heifer. Heifer answers to the fact that it is a feminine sacrifice for feminine failure. It has got to be slain, that life must be terminated to substitute for the living death of the daughter of Jerusalem that played the harlot against Jehovah—Thy Maker is thy husband! Or else it is the antitype slain as for the failure and deadness—thou hast a name to live and art dead—of the bride of Christ in this instance. I would say the red heifer had to come in again at Corinth: ye are yet carnal; awake thou that sleepest and arise from the dead! I would say the red heifer had to come in again when the law of sin and death came in in Galatians. I have espoused you as a pure virgin unto Christ, who hath beguiled you, who hath bewitched you? says Paul the apostle. You need a sacrifice to present before the Lord. Death come in? In this place? With a once living people? A red heifer.

As to the fact that it is without spot, if it had spot it could not be a sacrifice. If it had blemish, it could not answer to the blemish in another. It had to be a perfect substitute. And always the Lord's people must look out to and through a substitute. They must always come in Another, and appear in Another, even Christ. Who, as a Lamb without spot and without blemish, offered himself through the eternal Spirit spotless unto God to be the sacrifice for his people, that he might redeem them to God for his own worshipping and gathered saints. And there are sufficient merits in that all-redeeming death to answer to any contingency that comes into the church, so that she is not lost or fallen away by her decadence, or by her lack of virtue, or by her unfaithfulness, or by her deadness, but

27

that same sacrifice availeth; but it will bring them through it, and remind them of what it cost, their so lightly being faithless. And remind them of their common responsibility in the church to answer as a living people, as one body, as a bride unto her Lord and husband.

His super-abounding, over-abounding vigour, who ever liveth, who hath the dew of his youth in the beauties of holiness from the womb of the morning, who hath his life from out of his intrinsic divinity, his life is more than adequate for any death we will ever touch. There is nothing we can sink to in a way of deadness to the Spirit, deadness to God, deadness to the saints, that cannot be overcome by his life. And so 'death is swallowed up'. At Calvary he embodied it as a sacrifice, as a feminine counterpart for us in the church. Even though we have not touched death, he has given himself for when we do. The heifer was slain *before* death had come into the camp of God as a preparation for when it did. There is nothing we can do in a way of deadness with respect to the Father, the Son and the Holy Ghost for which this super-abounding life is not more than adequate. Romans 8: For I am persuaded that neither death nor life shall be able to separate us from the love of God which is in Christ Jesus our Lord ... not even death! John 8:51, Verily, verily, I say unto you, If a man keep my saying, he shall never see death.

And the last expression, 'upon which never came yoke', shows that it answers under the gospel. You ought not to be entangled again with the yoke of bondage, because the law worketh wrath. Sin comes by the law—I had not known sin, but by the law. And if you get legal, and under the legal yoke, why, then you will bring forth sin, because the law brings forth the knowledge of sin. And it works wrath. And therefore when sin comes forth, the judgment will be death. But upon this heifer no yoke came—she is a gospel heifer! It is a gospel substitute. And moreover, never came yoke—she never came by a way of works. She is no

Arminian heifer. She never worked. She did nothing but remain innocent.

This heifer is perceived in a way of faith. She is for them who are looking away by faith, not for them that are labouring away at works. If they want works, they have got to work their own salvation and get under the old yoke. But if you want grace, you must look away to a heifer who comes in no way of works: what you do, but in a way of grace: what he has done. But think not when you become dead and carnal or worldly in the church, or your church becomes dead and carnal and worldly, that it is as though your past belief and past faith once exercised suffice for this. Oh, no! It is experimental: the just shall *live* by faith; it is *from* faith *to* faith! And if you sin, you need immediately, then, an advocate. And your advocate must present the propitiatory sacrifice, as John clearly teaches you. You must see what it cost Christ. Not only to redeem you but to keep you. And you must keep your eyes upon Calvary's cross—for this is what it cost.

This heifer is a substitute for God's people in a general way, as for example, was the sin offering for ignorance. For ignorance was the sin that needed a sin offering in Israel. 'For if we sin wilfully after that we have received the knowledge of the truth, there remaineth no more sacrifice for sins.' It is wrong to minimise the force of such texts—if they will not receive the love of the truth, let them believe a lie. Therefore keep your vessel, the vessel of your body, unto sanctification, else the place begins to be and to feel defiled.

Our strength and help stand in a Priest on high, prayer below, a sword in the hand, a shield before, and the Spirit within. How wonderful to have Christ presiding over the church, keeping it clean! And what happens when death gets in among the Lord's people? It affects the whole church—'for this cause many are weak and sickly among you and many sleep.'

Now I say therefore that this vigorous red heifer stand-eth in Christ as a substitute for his bride—who gave himself for us that he might present us a pure and a holy bride, without spot or wrinkle. Husbands, love your wives, as Christ loved the church and gave himself for it; and in her place, in that sense, the heifer. So it is that for our dead defilement he is condemned to death in this sacrifice; as we see in Colossians 1:22, He reconciled us in the body of his flesh through death, to present us holy and unblameable and unreproveable in his sight. And moreover we see in 2 Tim. 1:10 that he hath abolished death, and brought life and immortality to light through the gospel. And Christ also overcame him who had the power of death, that is the devil, and took the keys from him, and now holds the keys, saying in the book of the Revelation in the first chapter, I have the keys of hell and of death. So that he has completely overcome in respect of death.

Indeed, it is true that all those who are in Christ are in a way of life by the Holy Ghost, for if any man have not the Spirit—mark that, *Spirit*—of Christ he is none of his. Those that at the first were able by the Spirit merely to open a flickering eyelid and look away to the cross in the weakest of little faith, who believed on the Lord Jesus Christ and were saved—the essence of their new birth—who in the regeneration looked away from themselves to a crucified Saviour, they look away to Christ, and hence it cometh to pass to all those that are in Christ what is said in John 5:24, He that believeth on him *has* passed from death unto life. And also what is said in John 8:51, He shall never see death.

And you ought never to see death, my brethren. And you ought never to bring death into the congregation of God's people. It is not a place for death. It is a place for life. You should feel it. 'Spring up, O well; sing ye unto it.' Moreover in Romans 6:9 I read, Death hath no more dominion. And furthermore in 1 Corinthians 15:54, I hear the apostle Paul say to me, Death, Metcalfe, death, he says, is swallowed up in victory! And I believe it, Paul. I believe you, my excellent mentor and teacher. Death is swallowed up in victory. Not petty half-hearted miserable defeat. Not half swallowed up. Not swallowed up in partial victory. Death is not half-regurgitated in victory. It is *swallowed up in victory*. And I understand from 2 Timothy 1:10 that Jesus Christ has abolished death.

You may say to me, But we still die. We still die, but I tell you, there is a difference. The unbeliever dies because of condemned sin, because of the curse upon the world in Adam, because he is under a certain fearful looking for of judgment that is already passed upon him, *and he will not come unto Christ that he might have life!* But the believer dies because this body is not his! He dies because he has to put it off. And that is the only reason he dies, otherwise every believer in the world that ever was would still be walking alive. But there is that in the body that he has got to put off. It is not that he dies, or need die, it is that this present body must be put off, that that body of glory be put on in due course.

There is the difference. Every unbeliever in this room dwells in his body alone. Every believer in this room, Christ dwells in him, the Father dwells in him and the Holy Ghost dwells in him, so he dwells in the body with God in Father, Son and Holy Ghost. As it is written, Ye are the temple of the living God; as God hath said, I will dwell in them and walk in them. And I tell you death makes no difference to God. He transforms the situation first by the substitutionary cross and then by the sanctifying indwelling.

Then you say to me, Why do we die? I answer, because still in the body is the body of sin. You say, Well, if we are in the body of sin, how can God dwell there? Because that sin was originally condemned in the body of Jesus on the tree, so that the believer is justified from sin as says the sixth chapter of Romans, even though he must still dwell in the body of it; because God's way of putting it off is through our actual bodily death, that he might raise the body again from the dead as a glorious body as he gloriously raised Christ from the dead, who was first as having been made sin for us put to death in the flesh, but sin being judged and put away in his death, God raised him from the dead! Christ is thus the firstfruits, then they that are Christ's at his coming.

So therefore there is this difference between the believer and the unbeliever. The unbeliever dies because he is damned and renounces the Lord of life, and will not come unto Christ that he might have life. The believer dies because this body is not his, because he has to put it off, because he has yet to put on Christ in this full and final sense. Therefore he must be planted together in the likeness of his death, that he might be raised together in the likeness of his resurrection. And because this world is not his. And just as Christ departed out of this world, so does the believer. Because this is not a believer's realm; he looks for a city, he looks for a world to come, he lives for another world and another age yet to be revealed at the coming of Christ.

You may object secondly, that since you die in the same way as unbelievers, it would appear believers and unbelievers are the same; and since they both have the same end in that sense, perhaps one could deceive oneself. I answer, Blessed in the sight of the Lord is the death of the righteous. And if you think they have the same end, you want to read some of the accounts I could recommend to you about the end of believers, and have a look at the end of unbelievers. Like the philosophising academic who raised his trembling hands to heaven, and cried, *More light!* as he passed from this life into the next. From death to death.

And you want to read the death of dear old Huntington, as he lay expiring in bed:

'You have suffered acutely,' they said. Replied he, 'I had worse pains once, with a burning ague, not a bed to lie on, and without an earthly comfort; but now I have every blessing in providence to alleviate my sufferings. My heart overflows with the goodness of God, and I lament being unable to find epithets sufficiently expressive to describe to others the sense I have of it.' Death held no terrors for him: 'All lies straight before me,' he said. 'There are no 'ifs' or 'buts'. I am as sure of heaven as if I were in it.'

Later, after complaining of the opposition he had met with throughout the whole of his ministry, and the hatred which he had experienced, not least from the professedly religious leaders, ministers and clergy, he said, 'Take a pen and write my epitaph: *"Here lies the Coalheaver, beloved of his God but abhorred of men. The Omniscient Judge at the Grand Assize shall ratify and confirm this to the confusion of many thousands, for England and the Metropolis shall know that there hath been a prophet among them."* '

Later he seemed to be sinking, the family was sent for; one said 'I am glad, sir, to see you look so comfortable.' 'Why should I look otherwise?' said Huntington. 'Death with me has lost its sting these forty years. I am no more afraid of death than I am of my nightcap!' Towards the evening he said, 'Oh bless his precious name!' and a little later, 'Why is his chariot so long in coming?' A storm was raging outside and he raised his head to listen. They told him the noise was caused by the hail outside lashing the window panes. The dying man turned back his head and tried to speak. Lady Sanderson heard him breathe 'Bless his precious name!' Then he gave a sigh and all was over.

One present remarked immediately 'Mark the perfect man, and behold the upright: for the end of that man is

33

peace.' But as to what he left behind him, then went down the sun on the generation to which he so faithfully testified, and then was removed the candlestick from that church, and the discerning could say 'Oh! What solemn news! Oh! What a severe loss!' But like this generation, the dead mass is indifferent to it, and sees and feels nothing but the passing of an irritant.

And, 'Ah,' he said, 'Bless his precious name!' And off he went. Off he went! Is it the same? Is death the same with the unrighteous? It might be the same in the body, but I tell you it is precious different in the soul. Fear not, Master Ridley!

First, it is different because of faith—faith in the word of God. You might say the bodies are the same, but internally the believer dies in faith. *These all died in faith* not having received the promises. But tell me one promise that has failed. Tell me one prophecy that has had the passage of time to travel to the foretold event, that has not come to pass! When a man cries a thousand years before it happened, 'They pierced my hands and my feet,' and he looked at his unblemished hands and his intact feet and wondered what was meant by it; yet he wrote it down because he felt in a mystery: God hath made me to say it. And three thousand years later you can look back two thousand years and see why. How can you doubt? And that is but one instance. I could multiply them many times over. I say, faith in the word of God shows that everything he says can be relied on and can carry you through. It is a bridge that shall never fail. It might sway, but it will not break. That is proved. And I say therefore, when you die in faith, you shall be raised in glory.

And secondly, because of hope. Now hope that is seen is not hope. It is not seen yet. But hope maketh not ashamed. And I assure you that he who dies in hope, his hope shall not make him ashamed. But yet in his flesh shall he see

34

God, and he shall stand at the latter day upon the earth, yea, though worms destroy this body, and though these bones turn to dust, in a moment, in the twinkling of an eye, at the last trump, the dead shall be raised incorruptible! Hope against hope! Is it a strange thing with you that God should raise the dead? He *has* raised the dead! Christ the firstfruits, then afterwards they that are his at his coming. Then hope shall cry in fulfilment, O death! where is thy sting? O grave! where is thy victory? Death is swallowed up in victory.

And thirdly, because of love. Because John says, Having loved his own, Jesus loved them unto the end. And do you think that a point is ever reached at which he lets us go? Is the end the point of our death? Do you think he loves us unto our end—when we die—and then turns away? I told you before and I tell you again, when you get to death and you are about to go and you can feel the darkness, and you begin to say, Who turned the light off? and they tell you that the light is still on: that through the darkness there will come a hand ready to grasp your hand and take you over. He loved them unto the end. And the end is not yet. For the end is in the glory. 'Then cometh the end, when he shall have delivered up the kingdom to God, even the Father.' And if you still doubt, then I can still give you one more salve from the balm of Gilead: saith the risen Lord: '*I am* Alpha and Omega, the beginning and *the end!*' If you must, wait and see! Wait and see ....!

To continue. In verse 4 of Numbers 19, we read that the priest shall take of the heifer's blood with his finger and sprinkle of her blood directly before the tabernacle of the congregation seven times. The finger speaks of precise, delicate, particular work: it is the digit used to exactitude; and sprinkled blood is blood disclosed globule by globule, as utterly to reveal every precious drop, it is seen of God to the ultimate worth. How exposed it all is! This is testimony before God. Death has taken place for death. And on that basis he sends the Mediator to conduct those once dead into a realm of life. Death is the antidote of death. 'Before the tabernacle of the congregation.' God is looking at his people across the sprinkling at this moment, ever-efficacious drops of blood once sprinkled from the finger of Christ: we are coming to the blood of sprinkling. Death for death. Life for life.

'And one shall burn the heifer in his sight; her skin, and her flesh, and her blood, with her dung, shall he burn.' This signifies getting to the root of inbred sin that brings forth death. Oh, this judges nature! This gets at the fall! Yet sings the Arminian perfectionist of sanctification: 'Thou shalt the root remove.' No; not in this life! Wesley's delusion of perfectionism was an error. The whole body of it must be judged, damned, condemned and burned in the substitutionary body of Jesus. It cannot be eradicated or removed from our persons in this life. The only way in which we will be freed from the body of sin and death is by the resurrection from the dead when 'we shall be changed!'

As long as we are here we will be in this vile body of inbred corruption, though blessed be God, it shall not have dominion over us, for we through the Spirit look for the hope of righteousness by faith, and as looking, feel that the Spirit of life in Christ Jesus hath made us free from the law of sin and death. Though as in this tabernacle it is true we do groan; but equally true we are kept, and kept mortified to the body of sin and death in a way of life through the Spirit: for if ye through the Spirit do mortify the deeds of the body ye shall live.

Then rather, look away to One who appeared before the bar of judgment at the cross and sunk under vindictive wrath at Calvary on your behalf, look, I say, to him to conduct your soul, and rejoice in the application of blood upon your soul from judgment upon his body, that in the faith therein ye should dwell in the Spirit. And if so be, for

36

the time, ye are in heaviness through manifold temptations, and if for a while you groan in this tabernacle, being burdened, and on occasions feel inbred sin stronger than the Spirit, yet this is the way of the flock. 'Now no chastening for the present seemeth to be joyous, but grievous: nevertheless afterward it yieldeth the peaceable fruit of righteousness unto them which are exercised thereby.' Chastisement brings down pride.

Look away to the funeral pyre, to the sacrifice of the red heifer, where Christ loved the church and gave himself for it. See how much is involved in a truly vicarious sacrifice: *Skin:* signifies not the actions done by the body—that would be the path taken, the footprints as it were—but what encloses the entire body. It encloses everything: take it off, all is exposed in its true underlying nature. Skin is all of outward appearance, all that men see: it is the greetings in the market place, it is the doing alms, the praying with a trumpet before one in the synagogues and in the streets, to have glory of man, it is to be seen of men; it is what covers up the flesh—that all its religion standeth not in secret before God but in public before men—but it must all be removed and judged!

Flesh: is what comes from Adam. It is man as he is in this present world, in this evil age, as under law, as of this creation, it indicates man in the realm of nature. Men from the fall, born of the flesh, born of the man of sin and death; seething, swarming, with the works thereof: lust, pride, envy, malice, avarice, fornication, uncleanness, inordinate affection, jealousy; O! how it swarms with the lust of the flesh, the lust of the eye and the pride of life, with the love of the world, of money, of covetousness, with the affections, desires, and passions; it must all go down in judgment, for that which is of the flesh is flesh.

Blood: this speaks of the life as pervaded by inbred sin, the life of nature, blood lineage. All the pride of genealogy, all the vaunted breeding of family, down to the very issues of life. But of blood, none shall be born of God; you may sit in your Anglican family pew in your swelling pride, but not many mighty, not many noble are called; you may trust in your circumcision and Jewish blood, or your Baptist father, or your Presbyterian ancestry, but it shall avail you nothing: flesh and blood cannot inherit the kingdom of God. It shall come down to judgment, and has, in the Substitute: blood!

Dung: all the stinking issue of the flesh; that which kept it alive and fed it is seen at the last for what it is: dung! It is a figure of what morally comes out of a man: 'the things which come out of him those are they that defile the man.' This is how what comes from within morally appears to the Holy One: he that hath ears to hear, let him hear. 'Yea doubtless, and I count all things but loss for the excellency of the knowledge of Christ Jesus my Lord: for whom I have suffered the loss of all things, and do count them but *dung*, that I may win Christ.' All things: all vaunted moral ethic, all religion, all legality: but dung. It is deathly, deathly, deathly.

'And the priest shall'—mark that, the priest shall: that is Christ; no usurper will do, Christ shall do it for you, and apply it to you, or you are under a lie; the priest, which in spirit is the Lord, shall—'take *cedar wood*.' Cedars are forever associated with Lebanon—the cedars of Lebanon are a byword. Mount Lebanon in appearance was white and snowy. If one stood on the flat plain and looked up to the mountains of Lebanon the heat-haze misted out the lower regions of the hills, and one could see almost a celestial land, heavenly, suspended, elevated—a kind of world to come that hung over this world, the snow peaks as it were hanging suspended towering over the land, so in a mystic picture Lebanon figured a heavenly country.

These cedars thereof were no earthbound Arminian saplings, wavy and frivolous; these were strong, solid,

38

stately, dignified trees! They are not conformed to all that grows from below, for they are of another kind than those formed on the plain beneath, on the lowly earth. These are the planting of the Lord, in a heavenly sphere, in an elevated realm; and it is so that a good tree bringeth forth good fruit. The house of God at Jerusalem was lined with cedar wood from Lebanon, with that wood from above; as surrounded by these, God dwells, for so it is that 'The righteous shall flourish like the palm tree: he shall grow like a cedar in Lebanon. Those that be planted in the house of the Lord shall flourish in the courts of our God.' That is it, they are the heavenly Father's planting. 'Trees of righteousness shall men call them' saith Isaiah, and says the psalmist, 'The trees of the Lord are full of sap; the cedars of Lebanon which he hath planted': these constituted his *living* house.

'And the priest—still the priest, notice—shall take *scarlet.*' Scarlet wool reminds us of the incident in Genesis 38 when Tamar was giving birth to twins. And as she travailed, one put out his hand, and the midwife bound a scarlet thread on his hand saying, This came out first. But he drew back his hand and his brother came out first. And afterward came out his brother that had the scarlet thread on his hand. And his name was called Zarah. Thus Zarah was an ancestor of Christ, promised before all yet not first to come; first in promise but second in the event.

So there was ever a Man in the mind of God, and though Adam came first, Christ had the scarlet thread. So also Cain was first, but Abel chosen; Esau was first, but Jacob was the elect. 'The first man Adam was made a living soul; the last Adam was made a quickening spirit. Howbeit that was not first which is spiritual, but that which is natural; and afterward that which is spiritual. The first man is of the earth, earthy: the second man is the Lord from heaven.' So the Lord of heaven put forth his hand out of eternity, created the worlds, then drew his hand back, and Adam

39

came first. But Christ the second man, the Lord of life, the life-giving Spirit, comes with no moral law but eternal life, with another manhood and another destiny. And his seed is in the first instance of heavenly planting—cedars, and secondly, in another man—scarlet wool, the mark of the living seed before God; Hear and your soul shall live!

'And the priest—the one only and alone Mediator—shall take *hyssop*.' Hyssop was that with which the blood was applied. It does no good to expatiate about the blood and its worth unless in experience one has got that blood applied to oneself within one's soul! *'Purge me* with hyssop, and I shall be clean; *wash me,* and I shall be whiter than snow.'

That there was a sacrifice made for redemption was one thing; that the great living High Priest should apply that to the people is another. That is what David recognises in Psalm 51. It is not enough to recognise the event of the sacrifice wrought of God—God must apply it. It is to *God* that David says, 'Purge me with hyssop,' Ps. 51:7. So also Heb. 9:19-20, 'For when Moses had spoken every precept to all the people according to the law, he took the blood of calves and of goats, with water, and scarlet wool, and hyssop, and sprinkled both the book, and all the people, saying, This is the blood of the testament which God hath enjoined unto you.' You see that it must be applied.

It is the Spirit that confirms the covenant's application to the people. He takes the things of Christ and in a living ministry shows them to us and applies them unto us. It is by hyssop that the blood is brought from the sacrifice to the suppliant. It is the grace of God that bringeth salvation: applies the blood. Says good old Mr. Hart:

> Sinners, I *read*, are justified,
> By faith in Jesus' blood;
> But when to me that blood's *applied*,
> 'Tis *then* it does me good!

40

It is to make a felt impact of the work that has been done, so as the soul is actually touched by it in power: hyssop is the type and figure of this work of the Holy Ghost.

David's son, who was wiser than all men, 'spake three thousand proverbs, and his songs were a thousand and five. And he spake of trees, from the cedar tree that is in Lebanon even unto the hyssop that springeth out of the wall.' Notice it does not say a wall, or any wall; it is *the* wall. And this wall spoken of by the King in Zion is the wall of Jerusalem; it hath foundations, wherein are the names of the twelve apostles of the Lamb. Since the hyssop springeth out of *that* wall, it can be said to signify the lively application of the doctrine of the apostles, upon which the walls of salvation are built.

For this hyssop grew out of that which rests upon the one foundation of apostolic doctrine in a figure, out of the walls of salvation in Zion, behind which had been brought the elect seed by the Holy Ghost. Therefore it signifies the application of that doctrine of the gospel on which the city of God stands, and as such it signifies the saving work of the Holy Ghost. It is God revealing these things unto us by the Spirit. It is the word coming in the Holy Ghost and with power to the inner man. It is the Spirit of the living God giving a lively ministry of the New Testament, not of the letter for the letter killeth, but of life and power to the soul, so as to feel the force of the very impact of the sacrificial blood upon and within oneself. The son of David understood the use of hyssop in its typical significance. What a wise man!

The means of applying redemption stands in the ministration of the Holy Ghost, it is by sanctification of the Spirit; neither is the election brought forth any other way than by the inward and experimental revelation that the Spirit gives of the burning wrath of God's righteousness—of which the blazing pyre of the sacrificed heifer was significant—met and vindicated in the death of Christ; here is the great sacrifice, where the fiery brands of heaven were quenched and the sevenfold vials of the fury and of the indignation of Almighty God were absorbed.

The church comes out of that death, as Eve came out of Adam in his deep sleep, for if she is to be one with the Man of life, she must be identified in his sufferings and in his death. And the Spirit is given to reveal and to apply the fruitful travail of Christ's soul—labour that came out of the hours on the cross when the judgment of God fell upon the Son of his love as he poured out his wrath on that sacrifice below. The elect see this by the Spirit in the crucified body of Jesus. At Calvary they see the fulfilment of every sacrifice, and it is there that they see a slain heifer burning, they see cedar wood, scarlet and hyssop cast in the burning, and know it is the price the Lord must pay, it is Christ loving the church—as a bride—and giving himself for her, it is judgment for trees that are planted of the heavenly Father, it is wrath taken in the second man for all the seed, it is fiery vengeance quenched for a people who shall afterwards be brought in by the administration of the Holy Ghost.

But when shall the virtue of the sacrifice, and what was consumed with it, be brought home to the needy soul? I answer, long, long after the fires are utterly exhausted! When nothing is left: nothing of either heifer herself, or her bones, neither her hoof, nor hide, nor yet the scarlet, nor the cedar wood, nor hyssop, nothing but a cone of cold dead ash—historically the event being past in time, the sacrifice once for all already over and finished—I say, *then* one shall take the ashes and lay them up outside the camp.

Lay them up: that is, lay up the present actual evidence of the past historical reality of the fact of there once having been a red heifer, lay up the memorial of the priestly sacrifice, lay up the record of a blood-letting in agonising death, lay up the testimony of the priestly sprinkling before the Lord at the door of the tabernacle, lay up the remains of a great fire kindled outside the camp, of the fact that once long ago there was the hurling of a carcase, of skin, flesh, blood and dung, into the roaring blaze, chronicle the fact that there was a casting in of cedar wood, scarlet and hyssop, write in a book that there was an utter consumption till all was that day reduced to ashes, consumed at the last to a cone of dead ash: a cone in which all that was long past is seen at present, and recorded in mind and memory by the true worshipper being recounted by the faithful priest. All this, which is in the ashes, is then taken and laid up outside the camp against the contingency of death defiling one within the camp in the future passage of time.

Whence it follows thereafter that if one of the congregation of the seed of Abraham, if an Israelite within the camp, be defiled by death either by touching the dead body of a man, or by entering into the tent of a man that has died, or by contact with the slain in the field, or by touching a bone of a man, or a grave—and I have shown the spiritual meaning of this—then if he count not himself unclean seven days, neither purify himself with the water of separation—and this with its content also I have expounded—on the third day after his defilement, then that soul shall be forever cut off from the congregation of the people of God: he shall be utterly excommunicated: it is a perpetual statute: he shall bear his uncleanness, it is upon him; he that is filthy let him be filthy still! The man that wandereth out of the way of understanding shall remain in the congregation of the dead: he abideth in death even until now.

But for the defiled person that will be clean even he shall pass a self-judgment upon his own defilement, and judge and condemn himself according to the judgment of God full seven days; for that perfect period—for the number seven when used in a figurative context indicates perfection —during which time the wages of sin, one's own sin, of defilement, one's own defilement, of unclean contamination, one's own uncleanness, is seen to bring death, death, and nothing but death, and seen to do so perfectly clearly, seen to do so to the end of the matter, clearly seen to be the unclean thing that defileth and so perceived, discerned and judged root and branch.

All the time it takes is taken, perfect time to bring total self-condemnation and utter abhorrence of that which defileth. No superficial judgment of a temporary symptom is given, but the uttermost cause is judged, because the full period needed to expose the evil perfectly before the penitent is required by him that hath abolished death and brought life and immortality to light through the gospel.

On the third day of the seven, the third since the Israelite was defiled by death, then it is that the unclean person shall purify himself with the waters of separation. Notwithstanding the remaining four days he shall ponder the cost to the heifer, the price of cedar, scarlet, and hyssop! Thus that which he counted so lightly—that deadness which he brought into the congregation with such ease and toleration —is seen to be the same as that which God set so vast a price upon, and which caused the Most High to stand aghast at the foulness, filthiness and uncleanness thereof, till nothing but blood, death, judgment and fiery conflagration could satisfy his righteousness.

Hence the signification of the third day is that Christ loved the church—as a husband loveth his wife—and gave himself for it that he might sanctify and cleanse it by the washing of water through the Word; moreover that three days he lay dead, and by his dying death was vanquished— for in the mouth of two or three witnesses every matter is established—and the third day he rose victorious from the dead, and death was swallowed up in victory. Thus the third day is the day on which it could be said, O death, where is thy sting? O grave, where is thy victory? Death is swallowed up in victory! But at what cost the living should ponder full seven days, with particular emphasis upon the third day.

Now therefore for the unclean person that will be clean, on this significant day, the third day, they shall take of the ashes of the burnt heifer of purification for sin, with all the memorial therein contained, and this 'shall be put ... in a vessel.' Being 'put within a vessel' signifies that the full truth, doctrine and reality of the death as bearing on carnal deadness and contact therewith is brought home and laid up in mind and heart inwardly.

For the teaching is that the memorial and record of the death, the gathered up ashes signifying the satisfaction of God's righteousness in the uttermost demands of judgment, must as such be put into and enclosed within the vessel. This demonstrates to the penitent what he must contain within himself, in his own bodily vessel; it typifies the internal reception of the truth of the death of Christ for that elect vessel the church, a vessel of the resurrection, a vessel unto honour, a chosen vessel unto God, for it is a figure on the third day to show that we have this treasure of the precious doctrine of the cross and resurrection put within the earthen vessel. Yes, we have this treasure in earthen vessels, contained and laid up in the interior of the soul; it is a figure of 'ye obeyed from the heart the form of doctrine delivered unto you', precious treasure deposited within the heart of our vessels, that every man should know how to possess his vessel unto sanctification.

But this is far from the whole: for together with the ashes enclosed in the vessel—the meaning of which we have seen—'running water shall be put thereto.' This running water signifies the person and work of the Holy Ghost: for he that believeth on Christ, as the scriptures hath said, out

45

of his belly shall flow rivers of living water: this spake he of the Spirit.

To bring the defiled person to self-judgment the Spirit had before awakened, alarmed and convicted him so that three days he had mourned apart and bewailed his offensiveness to God and obnoxiousness to his wrath. But now in a quickening work the washing of regeneration and renewing of the Holy Ghost is shed upon him abundantly through Jesus Christ his Saviour.

I say, this running water signifieth the Holy Ghost, the One that came to the saints from a view of the death of Christ ... 'they saw that Jesus was dead already, and they brake not his legs, but one of the soldiers with a spear pierced his side, and forthwith came there out blood and water.' By the washing of water through the Word, the Holy Ghost brings that historical death of Jesus—in the written and laid up memorial thereof—in living, running and flowing power to the defiled, and brings the unclean to that death in the same power of a life-giving ministration of the Spirit. So comes to pass the saying, That day there shall be a fountain opened to the house of David and to the inhabitants of Jerusalem for sin and for uncleanness; then will I sprinkle clean water upon you and ye shall be clean from all your filthiness; I will also save you from all your uncleannesses, saith the LORD.

Thus to the plea of David, Wash me throughly from mine iniquity and cleanse me from my sin; and again, Purge me with hyssop and I shall be clean, wash me and I shall be whiter than snow: God replieth, When the Lord shall have washed away the filth of the daughters of Zion, and shall have purged the blood of Jerusalem from the midst thereof by the spirit of judgment and by the spirit of burning: yea, I say, God replieth: Then washed I thee with water, yea, I throughly washed away thy blood from thee; so that now it can be affirmed through the washing of water by the

Word, by the washing of regeneration, that which the apostle Paul saith to the Corinthian church: But ye are washed, but ye are sanctified, but ye are justified in the name of the Lord Jesus, and by the Spirit of our God! This is good measure pressed down and running over, and well might David say, when washed in the running waters of the washing of regeneration and renewal of the Holy Ghost, My cup runneth over.

What follows now is the taking of this vessel in which running water has mingled to overflowing with the ashes of the burnt heifer, with the cedar wood and hyssop and scarlet, and this vessel is carried on the third day to the tent; then a clean person must take hyssop and dip it in the water and sprinkle the tent, all the vessels, all the persons that were there and all that was defiled. 'And the clean person shall sprinkle upon the unclean on the third day and on the seventh day: and on the seventh day he shall purify himself and wash his clothes and bathe himself in water, and shall be clean at even.' Notice that so defiling is death in the natural, carnal sense, and so hateful to the Lord of life that even the clean person who touched the water of separation must needs wash his clothes and remain unclean until the even. But to return.

I say, it is the running water that brings efficacy to ashes, brings unction to doctrine, brings in the demonstration of the Spirit and of power, brings preaching that is not in word only but in power also; it is the Spirit that quickeneth, it must be in words which the Holy Ghost teacheth, the truth must be anointed; yes, there must be the running water, and the running water must be seen to run generally upon and in the whole church so that the church is seen to be the vessel of the Holy Ghost.

Yet notwithstanding, for personal cleansing even more especial grace is needed! For hyssop must be taken for special and precise application. 'Shall take hyssop and dip it in the water and shall sprinkle upon the unclean.' It is not only a belief in the doctrine of it, however internal that may be; it is not merely a sight of the mighty working of the Spirit in demonstration and in power, however that may be in evidence; all that is already seen in and deduced from the vessel full of mingled running water and ashes.

But now a *further* thing is seen! It is the hyssop taken in addition to the full vessel withal that this teaches, and taken so as to splash *oneself!* It is not the sight of ashes, running water, or the vessel being brought therewith; it is not the three days of mortifying and penitent self-judgment; but it is the taking of hyssop and by it bringing water from the vessel to the penitent, I say it is *that* which brings cleansing in the third and last analysis! It is 'Purge *me* with hyssop and *I* shall be clean.' It is particular: power to each and every individual precisely, for hyssop is taken to apply the water in particular, to each singular individual in person and personally.

Thus in the vessel with the ashes mixed with running water we see the blending of the word of the cross with the living Spirit in moving renewing sanctifying power: this is then sprinkled with hyssop upon the man to be cleansed, coming home to his person with all the felt and experienced impact of that water of separation splashing and soaking all down the dripping man, who is the picture of the restored child of God under the sensible experience of the embrace of and union with the risen Christ in the filling of the Holy Ghost, who weeps with adoring gratitude as lost in wonder, love and praise, and crying as we may suppose 'Oh wonder, why such love to me?'

What a deliverance! What restoration! What experimental religion! Yet we must never forget that before such a restoration, before the Holy Ghost could come with moving power and bring in a people, that first the people must as before God and in justice go down into death, yea, into fiery oblivion! and this through a living and dying vicarious Substitute. Wherever they look this is before their eyes! He who would look into election must look at it through the flaming wrath which Christ quenched for the deliverance of his people in his own body at the cross. He who would know the ways of the Spirit, and have the Spirit, must look at the fiery incandescence where in the vivid blaze is outlined the crumbling skeleton of the once-slain heifer. *Keep your eye on that death!*

It is in Jesus' death on the cross, with flowing blood that running water is seen; and he that saw it bare record, and his record is true, and he knoweth that he saith true, that ye might believe. The Holy Ghost is received by the believer under the hearing of faith in Christ crucified. 'And I, brethren, when I came to you ... determined not to know anything among you save Jesus Christ and him crucified. And I was with you in weakness and in fear and in much trembling. And my speech and my preaching was not with enticing words of man's wisdom, but in demonstration of the Spirit and of power: that your faith should not stand in the wisdom of men, but in the power of God.'

It is the 'running water' that brings efficacy to the gospel, unction to the Word, and anointing upon the testimony. The Holy Ghost fell on all them that believed. They preached with the Holy Ghost sent down from heaven. The present unction and living energy of the blessed Holy Spirit is what is signified by 'running water'. The sensible power and presence of the Holy Ghost in the church—they were all filled with the Holy Ghost—and on the preaching—with great power gave the apostles witness of the resurrection—so that it is clear, that here is a Spirit-filled people, a church of indwelling risen life, here is apostolic preaching, unction upon the Word, anointing upon the gospel: it can be seen. It is not the dead letter which killeth, but the life-giving ministration of the Spirit. This is 'running water' in a vessel with 'the ashes of an heifer'.

But if seen collectively, individually it must be applied! The hyssop is that especial, particular and precise application to the singular, sole and individual person so as to bring in *that* person to these things. It is hyssop that takes the running water and ashes in the vessel and brings that home to the individual. It is *that* work of the Spirit not in others, not in the church in general, but *to me*, which brings the soul to the cross and the cross to the soul by this living and felt application. It is the immediate present power and vital energy of the Holy Ghost to apply, to bring home the wonderful treasure deposited. The sprinkling signifies the actual application and consequent closing of the soul therewith.

Thus the Holy Ghost is shed abroad in the heart, a spirit of wisdom and revelation is given in the knowledge of Christ, the illuminating, life-giving, love-imparting, soul-quickening work comes in with sensible power to the inner man, rivers of water well up unto everlasting life, the well is sprung up and the heart-melody begins to it, the anointing, earnest, sealing, and renewing of the Spirit bears witness with the soul that it is brought into a living place indeed, and in a vital and quick company the Holy Ghost leads into all truth, brings all things to remembrance, and constantly affirms Christ's glory, speaks of him, and magnifies his holy name within the church that is in God the Father and in the Lord Jesus Christ.

This is the work that brings in that people—and of the rest durst no man join himself unto them—whom the Lord adds to the church; this is Christ building *his* church, which is no dead dry formal church, no worldly congregation, no denominational sect, but the church of the living God, the temple of the Holy Ghost, the indwelt house of God, the body of Christ. This work brings in the soul that is gathered to the congregation of his saints. This is the people that shall live before the Lord. This the company for whom he died, that once-purchased people whom the Holy Ghost has called and whom he indwells as a whole, and to which by a felt vital sensible application he brings in such as shall be saved and such as shall be restored: brings them in, I say, to the living company, one by one from out of the wilderness and death of this sentenced and condemned world. Of these is constituted the church of the living God, the pillar and ground of the truth, the house of God not made with hands, the temple of the Holy Ghost: this is the living, the living, that shall praise thee this day, and it is here, in spiritual Zion, that God commands the blessing, even life for ever more! O! The Lord bless the Word! Amen and Amen.

Now whoso is wise, and will observe these things, even they shall understand the loving kindness of the LORD.

CURRENT BOOKLIST

Obtainable from the publishers

TITLES:

NOAH AND THE FLOOD   *new series*   *£1.20*

"Mr. Metcalfe makes a skilful use of persuasive
eloquence as he challenges the reality of one's
profession of faith ... he gives a rousing call to a
searching self-examination and evaluation of one's
spiritual experience."

The Monthly Record of the Free Church of Scotland.

"In an age which claims to put the practical accent on
Christian interpretation of scripture, it is refreshing
to go back and look at the spiritual meaning in the
Bible. We need some forceful reminder that refuge
may be found in the Ark."

The Catholic Fireside.

"Noah and the Flood is an excellent exposition of
the story of Noah found in Genesis chapters 6-9.
No one reading this book can fail to be stirred by the
author's challenging and heart-searching exposition."

Dr. A. J. Monty White.

"Many will appreciate the original thought and
clarity of expression and the application to the
individual today."

Dr. F. Tatford (Prophetic Witness).

DIVINE FOOTSTEPS   *40p*

Divine Footsteps traces the pathway of the feet of
the Lord the Son of man from the very beginning in
the prophetic figures of the true in the Old Testament
through the reality in the New; doing so in a way of
experimental spirituality. At the last a glimpse of the
coming glory is beheld as his feet are viewed as
standing at the latter day upon the earth.

"Originality of thought and approach is apparent."

The Expository Times.

THE RED HEIFER   *new series   75p*

This book has been edited from a powerful sermon
preached by John Metcalfe in Tylers Green Chapel.
The verbal directness makes the book very readable
and simple to understand.

The Red Heifer was the name given to a sacrifice
used by the children of Israel in the Old Testament
— as recorded in Numbers chapter 19 — in which a
heifer was slain and burned. Cedar wood, hyssop and
scarlet were cast into the burning, and the ashes
were mingled with running water and put in a vessel.
It was kept for the children of Israel for a water of
separation: it was a purification for sin.

In this unusual book the sacrifice is brought up to
date and its relevance to the church today is shown.

THE WELLS OF SALVATION   *new series   £1.50*

The Wells of Salvation is written from a series of
seven powerful addresses preached at Tylers Green
Chapel. It is a forthright and experimental exposition
of Isaiah 12:3, 'Therefore with joy shall ye draw
water out of the wells of salvation.'

We quote:

John Metcalfe, acknowledged to be 'perhaps the most
gifted expositor and powerful preacher of our day'
nonetheless possesses a controversial challenge in his
ministry which presses home long-ignored issues in a
way 'which cannot be ignored'.

This is to be seen clearly in The Wells of Salvation,
in and of itself a unique and richly rewarding study
worthy of the reader's careful attention.

"Among truly great Christian works."

Methodist review.

"Outstanding."

The English Churchman.

"Impressive."

The Life of Faith.

TRACTS:

The Two Prayers of Elijah . . . .

'Tract for the Times' series:

1. The Gospel of God . . . .

2. The Strait Gate . . . .

3. Eternal Sonship and Taylor Brethren . . .

THE TWO PRAYERS OF ELIJAH

10p

This tract, first printed in 1972, was reprinted in 1975. It shows the spiritual significance of the drought, the cloudburst, and the two prayers of Elijah.

THE GOSPEL OF GOD

stiff cover, 25p

Tract for the Times 1

Beautifully designed, this tract positively describes the gospel under the following headings: The Gospel is of God; The Gospel is Entirely of God; The Gospel is Entire in Itself; The Gospel is Preached; The Gospel Imparts Christ; and, Nothing But the Gospel Imparts Christ. The last two headings also expose the recent moves to undermine the truth that Christ is conveyed simply through the gospel.

"It takes the discernment of an utterly fearless man like John Metcalfe to tear the mask off the moves that are taking place in the high circles of the church today. Here are 48 pages of verbal dynamite exposing the way in which the evangelical faith is being undermined by the statements of the Anglican-Roman Catholic Commission in its pronouncements concerning the meaning of the eucharist, the priestly and sacrificial character of the ministry, and papal authority."

From the comment of a Methodist minister.

THE STRAIT GATE

stiff cover, 25p

Tract for the Times 2

Exceptionally well made, this booklet consists of extracts from 'The Messiah', compiled in such a way as to challenge the shallowness of much of today's 'easy-believism', whilst positively pointing to the strait gate.

Eternal Sonship and Taylor Brethren
Tract for the Times No. 3
Price 25p

has now been published,

45 pages, with special stiff gloss finished cover featured in this high quality series.

This booklet is highly recommended, particularly for those perplexed by James Taylor's teaching against the eternal sonship of Christ.

This teaching impugnes the doctrine of J.N. Darby and his colleagues, denies the teaching of the Reformation, and refuses the orthodox preaching of the person of Christ throughout the ages. Besides this it recants upon the earlier ministry of Taylor himself. Above all, James Taylor's latter teaching against the eternal sonship of Christ contradicts the faith once delivered to the saints, and defies the apostles' doctrine, denying what has always been held about the eternity of Father, Son and Holy Ghost.

In a day when the term 'believer' is used so lightly that the vast majority think of it as barely related to *what* one believes — although in fact what one believes gives the only true title to the term 'believer' — this Tract for the Times thoroughly searches out truth from error, the believer from the infidel, the true Christ from the false, and leaves the reader in no doubt whatsoever as to the issue.

'APOSTOLIC FOUNDATION

OF THE CHRISTIAN CHURCH':

Vol. 1, Foundations Uncovered . . . . . .

Vol. 2, The Birth of Jesus Christ . . . . . .

Vol. 3, The Messiah . . . .

Vol. 4, The Son of God and Seed of David . .

FOUNDATIONS UNCOVERED   *30p*
Volume 1

Foundations Uncovered is a small book of some 37 pages. This is the Introduction to the major series: 'The Apostolic Foundation of the Christian Church'.

Rich in truth, the Introduction deals comprehensively with the foundation of the apostolic faith under the descriptive titles: The Word, The Doctrine, The Truth, The Gospel, The Faith, The New Testament, and The Foundation.

The contents of the book reveal: The Fact of the Foundation; The Foundation Uncovered; What the Foundation is not; How the Foundation is Described; and, Being Built upon the Foundation.

Our reviewer states:

"This book comes with the freshness of a new Reformation.

"In this Introduction, the author sets out the exhaustive method of arriving at the knowledge of the apostolic doctrine of the Christian faith.

"He outlines that objective body of truth which sets forth the Son of God, and which is the only valid foundation on which the church is built."

THE BIRTH OF JESUS CHRIST

new series 95p

Volume 2

"The author expresses with great clarity the truths revealed to him in his study of holy scripture at depth. We are presented here with a totally lofty view of the Incarnation.

"This is a fascinating and enlightening study. The author's examination of Biblical material is the reverent approach of someone who recognises the living quality of God's Word, and who waits to be instructed from it without pre-determining his own attitude.

"The very spirit of adoration and worship rings through these pages. In this new section of his work 'The Apostolic Foundation of the Christian Church', there is again indication that John Metcalfe is to be classed amongst the foremost expositors of our age; and although the value of his contribution to Christian thought may not yet be acclaimed, his writings have about them that quality of timelessness that makes me sure they will one day take their place among the heritage of truly great Christian works."

From a review by Rev. David Catterson.

"A book to be studied ... an outstanding contribution."

The English Churchman.

"Uncompromisingly faithful to scripture ... has much to offer which is worth serious consideration ... deeply moving."

The Expository Times.

"A thoroughly orthodox outlook ... impressive."

The Life of Faith.

THE MESSIAH
new series   £2.45
Volume 3

"This is no ordinary book. It is extraordinary, judged by the standards of godly doctrine in any age, and especially so when compared to the comparative impoverishment of the modern pulpit and pen. I firmly believe that it will be treasured as a spiritual classic by people not yet born.

"It draws out the inwardness of the beatitudes in a truly experimental way. It faithfully warns of judgment to come; with alarming descriptions of the Great Day. Law and gospel are distinguished, yet both honoured. Outstanding are the passages dealing with the threefold temptation of Jesus; and the Baptist's threefold description of the Messiah's work. What glorious light breaks out of the saying, 'Suffer it to be so now: for thus it becometh us to fulfil all righteousness.'

"It bears throughout the stamp of true ministry, raised up of GOD, not in letter but touching the spirit, bearing life. It comes from one who has been on his face, eaten the roll, and spoken only after sitting down seven days, (Ezekiel ch. 3) and the LORD'S people, whether they will hear or whether they will forbear (for they are a rebellious people) yet shall know that there hath been a prophet among them."

David Hughes, B.Sc., M.B., Ch.B.

"Its author is clearly a great lover of the Bible."

Maurice Nassan S.J., Catholic Herald.

"Something of the fire of the ancient Hebrew prophet ... Metcalfe has spiritual and expository potentials of a high order."

The Life of Faith.

The Son of God and Seed of David

Vol. 4 in the work entitled

The Apostolic Foundation of the Christian Church.

J.M.P.T.

250 pages

Hand-made in England.

£1.10

from your bookseller

or

the Publishing Trust at Tylers Green Chapel, Tylers Green Penn, Buckinghamshire, England.

REVIEW

'DOCTRINE ON FIRE'

'The Son of God and Seed of David' by John Metcalfe

A Review by Dr. David Hughes

As with the earlier volumes, the reader feels that this man has kept company with Christ and his holy apostles, and is sent directly to our age to expose the glaring disparity between modern Christianity and theirs, to root out and to pull down, to destroy and to throw down, thence-forward to build up and to plant.

The author, opening and alleging that Jesus Christ is and ever was THE SON OF GOD, brings proof after proof and furnishes scripture upon scripture, with overwhelming effect. Who can withstand this avalanche of undeniable evidence?

This greatest of subjects, this most profound of all mysteries, is handled with reverence and outstanding perception.

From plumbing such depths, the book turns to the consideration of THE SEED OF DAVID. A wealth of divine enlightenment appears. Reaching to magnificence, we now behold David the man, David the heir, and David the king. This flows, page after page, seraphic and sublime. Passages soar in eloquence; heights are scaled as the truth is unfolded with piercing clarity.

Finally, as the majesty of Christ is revealed, a crescendo is reached and it appears just how near the last Day we are, as the fast-moving events of the twentieth century are prophetically and penetratingly analysed.

On laying down 'The Son of God and Seed of David' one reaches this inescapable conclusion: Here is doctrine on fire.

David Hughes, B.Sc., M.B., Ch.B.

ORDER FORM:

(see overleaf)

INCREASED PRICES

When first the Trust was raised up, we printed and bound
all our own books, passing on to the public little more than
the cost of paper and ink. Freely we had received, freely
we gave.

Now it has pleased God so to bless this work that no longer
are we able to meet the demands for our books by the small
and laborious hand-processing with which we began the
work.

Therefore, having sold out of most of our stocks, we are
obliged to fulfil present and future orders by having our
books made by the up-to-date methods of professional
printers elsewhere, and hence the considerable price rise.

Our principles however remain the same: not only are these
reprinted titles passed on to the public at less than cost, but
all of us at the Trust give you our services without money and
without price. As always, there are no royalties or publisher's
costs relayed to the public by the John Metcalfe Publishing
Trust.

Why not? Because we seek our own benefit? God knoweth,
we seek not our own, not yours but you, that you may be
blessed from God the Father by Jesus Christ our Lord, in the
free knowledge of the gospel of the grace of God.

'Thanks be unto God for his unspeakable gift.'

ORDER FORM

Quantity

Noah and the Flood . . . . £1.20 + *21p* ☐

Divine Footsteps . . . . 40p + *14p* ☐

The Red Heifer . . . . 75p + *14p* ☐

The Wells of Salvation . . . . £1.50 + *29p* ☐

The Two Prayers of Elijah . . . . 10p + *8p* ☐

The Gospel of God . . . . 25p + *11p* ☐

The Strait Gate . . . . 25p + *11p* ☐

Eternal Sonship and Taylor Brethren . . 25p + *11p* ☐

Foundations Uncovered . . . . 30p + *14p* ☐

The Birth of Jesus Christ . . . . 95p + *21p* ☐

The Messiah . . . . £2.45 + *60p* ☐

The Son of God and Seed of David . £1.10 + *37p* ☐

(Figures in italics show postage & packing) *

NAME AND ADDRESS (in block capitals)

— —

— —

— —

Enclose remittance with order.
Cheques payable to 'The Publishing Trust'.

* *Postage costs are correct at time of going to press, and apply to
the U.K. only.*

cut here